SUCCEEDING IN YOUR POSITION

TEN ESSENTIAL INGREDIENTS FOR SUCCESS

DREXWELL SEYMOUR

Halo Publishing International
7550 WIH-10 #800, PMB 2069,
San Antonio, TX 78229

First Edition, May 2023
ISBN: 978-1-63765-370-8
Library of Congress Control Number: 2023902051

Dedicated to all the individuals who have taken the challenge to rise up and take their position. Now that you have taken your position, it is important for you to succeed in your position. Therefore, this book is for you.

Contents

Introduction

Success should be one of our primary goals in life. If that is your goal, this book is for you.

In 2021, my first book, *Rise Up and Take Your Position,* was published. Pretty much defined by the title, my purpose in writing it was to assist others in finding their place in life.

What is your purpose in life, your reason for being? Have you ever stopped and thought about the question, why am I here? I genuinely believe that we all have a purpose. The question then becomes are we fulfilling this purpose?

Together, let's search for the right path toward finding our primary purpose in life, and I hope my words can give you some thoughts for reflection.

When you find your WHY, you don't hit Snooze! Instead, you find a way to make it happen!

Everyone has a particular place in this world; no one is born and nothing is made by God without a reason. A man should always search for the purpose with which he was born. Once he finds that specific place and purpose of his life, he should start moving forward to take the next step, and that is the path or journey that will lead him to success.

If a person, in whatever place or with whatever purpose in his life, has an idea about how to achieve success, my belief is that you should not wait for the right moment. It might never come. If you want to succeed—either in your relationships, in your life, or in your career—you have to work for it; it is up to you to make those moments right for your success.

Understanding purpose is one thing, but recognizing the importance of having purpose is another.

Success

But, first, let's discuss success and how it's related to finding your purpose in life!

Feeling successful and purposefully living are essential in any stage of life.

We frequently define success as having wealth, and when we do not, we consider ourselves failures. However, success is more than just money; it is about achieving your life's goals and purpose.

We often see in our daily lives that for many people—it could be one of your friends, family members, or even you—the primary goal of life is to accumulate wealth in a short period of time. Isn't that so?

So hear me out: if that's your sole purpose of living, or if you consider being wealthy your end goal, then you must start working to achieve it. You have found the purpose in your life, you know your place, and you should now work to achieve your goal!

However, according to 1 Timothy 6:10 (New International Version), "the love of money is a root of all kinds of evil." Moreover, even if you become wealthy, you can still feel as if something is lacking. This means that you still haven't achieved your full potential, the real purpose of why you were born, and the exact purpose for your life. But once you understand the actual meaning of your life, you will experience ultimate inner peace, and every battle within yourself will settle down eventually. Once you achieve the success you have been looking for your whole life, the money will come to you quickly.

To emphasize this particular thought and idea more, let's recall Proverbs 18:16.

> ***A gift opens the way and ushers the giver into the presence of the great.***

History has shown that there are many people who can be our accurate life role models, people who are great examples of success.

The second main essence of success is having the Lord's acceptance of your lifestyle.

Let's look at the lives of Joseph and Daniel. I always considered them successful beings in everything.

Why? Because they had Lord on their side. The Lord always had Joseph's and Daniel's backs in everything they did because they gave of their time and dedicated themselves to Him. They obeyed His words and His teachings with pure intentions.

If you or I want God's ultimate help on our path toward success, then we must act on His words. We must do what Joseph and Daniel did: meditate, pray, and obey God. Never forget 1 Corinthians 3:7.

> ***So neither the one who plants nor the one who waters is anything, but only God, who makes things grow.***

Not everyone is able to pinpoint their life's purpose. You will be leading the kind of life you believe you were destined to lead once you decide to go after it. Additionally, you will be content. I believe that knowing your life's purpose is the first step toward living a truly conscious life. A life purpose provides us with a clear goal, a set finish line that we genuinely want to reach.

> ***The two most important days in your life are the day you are born and the day you find out why.***
>
> ***(Mark Twain)***

If you're searching for where you should start, start within yourself. Search for the meaning of your life. God has made you with a purpose, and it is hidden somewhere within you; what you have to do is search for it within yourself. Search for it, and win that part of yourself. God has a purpose for everything, and it's a good and correct purpose that will end up giving us fuller love and compassion from the heart of God. He wouldn't have hidden it from you if He did not want you to learn the true meaning behind your coming to this Earth.

One more thing that can take you a step forward toward your success and goals is never leaving your plans unattended; in other words, never delay what you're planning to do. Take that risk you always wanted to take, and make that move you constantly strategized to have.

If you write down your journey and plan every move, all of this could be possible. Because documenting your goals to pursue your purpose is not old school. It indicates that you are organized and tells a lot about your passion for your end goal.

Most of you have probably, at some time or other, have become easily discouraged when you did not get the desired income or whenever there was a delay in any of God's plans. Believe me, this is a normal reaction for every human. You may easily get discouraged if you do not see the physical manifestation of your goals.

But God has told us multiple times that we shouldn't ever get discouraged when experiencing hard times; we will eventually get the success for which we are working.

When you pass through the waters, I will be with you; and when you pass through the rivers, they will not sweep over you. When you walk through the fire, you will not be burned; the flames will not set you ablaze.

(Isaiah 43:2)

If things do not work for you one day, start working on it with the same enthusiasm the next day. Then, if you fail again, it's not too late to start anew. Life may give you a challenging time and some obstacles, but the key to a successful life is always to stay focused on the end goal and never let anything come between you and your dream life.

Often, amid everything, we realize that the things we are passionate about might be unattainable. But we should never take a step back. It is time for us to be brave and to work hard to live the life of our dreams according to our vision and purpose, instead of the expectations and opinions of others. We see proof of this belief in Proverbs 13:4.

A sluggard's appetite is never filled, but the desires of the diligent are fully satisfied.

To achieve a successful life, you must make sacrifices, because to earn something, you must learn to sacrifice those things closest to your heart. Also, your wisdom can lead you to new heights and places, so always be well equipped with good knowledge and plenty of information about current trends.

To determine your success, look within yourself for your life's purpose on this planet. Set realistic and measurable goals to achieve your goals once you've discovered your purpose. It is feasible to attain the sense that God has placed within you. Use this as your guide to accomplishing your objectives. You must have faith while also working hard to achieve your goals.

You have to remember that everyone's life is different. So believe in yourself because you are unique. There is something special about you. It's time for you to discover your uniqueness, hone it, and become successful.

Questions for discussion

1. Who are the successful people in your life? Can you name the things they did to achieve success?
2. Do you know your purpose in life? Write it down. Keep it with you.
3. List your goals right now. They may change when you finish this book.
4. List the steps you need to achieve your goals—education, money, promotion, etc.

> “Be yourself today. Compete with not another soul. It’s hard to stay in your lane when you’re looking everywhere else but forward.”

(Unknown Author)

Chapter 1

Stay in Your Lane!

The First Ingredient for Success

It's simple to assess other people's success and compare it with your own circumstances. But when you are still settling into life, you can observe people who appear to have everything worked out and possess the ideal career, home, and relationships.

An excellent technique to avoid comparison anxiety is to stay in your lane. Staying in your lane allows you to cross the finish line so that you fulfill your purpose. Focus your attention on yourself, rather than looking at everyone else's successes and failures. Everyone actually has a distinctive chronology that is all their own. Some people meet their soulmates when they are still in their teens, while others discover them much later in life. Every road is unique; there is no right or wrong.

The ideal will always be to live our lives as we see fit. Sadly, this has become so difficult in modern society because we've grown accustomed to continually comparing ourselves to others.

This type of thinking may have gotten the better of you as well. But, remember, we are not required to compare ourselves to others. We must recognize that each of us leads a unique life and that several avenues, routes, and orientations are available to us. So, instead of focusing on others' journeys, stay in your lane and mind your own business.

The path you need to walk would be a lot more obvious if you did this, and your chances of getting lost would be quite low because you will have kept your attention on yourself and experienced life to the fullest.

To illustrate, athletes must stay in their lane on the playing field if they want to have a shot at winning a medal. They lose points if they somehow stray from their lanes. Let's take the example of Delano Williams of the Turks and Caicos; he competed in an Olympic relay team for Great Britain. The entire nation of Turks and Caicos was ecstatic because his squad was set to win a medal. Sadly, the team was disqualified after the race was reviewed because one of the team members had crossed into the wrong lane. The team would have been successful if that individual had been attentive and stayed in his lane.

Each of us has a race that has been designated. Once you've identified it, run it with tenacity, and you'll triumph. To avoid getting distracted, stay in your lane and avoid looking to the side to see how others are faring. To win the race, remain concentrated and keep looking straight ahead. Though you may get worn out, keep going. Go on rushing for the goal. We should all settle at our own pace and not think about what others are doing with their lives.

Be Yourself—No Limitations

Another lesson that comes from this is staying out of other people's business and not imitating them. It would help if you weren't enticed to see what others are doing because it will always become a distraction and divert you from your goals. Also, always believe in yourself, as it will keep you and your identity unique because, by imitating others, you cannot achieve what they are gaining in their lives.

Sometimes we copy others and are attracted to those who seem successful. We behave similarly —we walk, talk, and dress the same way—and we strive to achieve the same goals they did. By copying others, you might make some money, but you won't have fun.

You Are Unique

Stop copying other people. You are endowed with your own special talent. Maintain your focus, practice your gift, and find happiness. You are on the path to success if you are content. There will be space for you.

Your uniqueness lies in not imitating others' lives because imitation and comparison are the most toxic elements in the human heart; they destroy ingenuity and rob you of peace and joy. Our unique self is empowered, powerful, and unstoppable! Our uniqueness is what makes us incomparable! We should not underestimate the beauty of just being ourselves.

We don't have to put our confidence in some deified Spiritual Superman's shoulders or wait for Fate to arrive at our door. Simply believing in and using our innate power is all that is required. Things start to go our way when we cease copying others and rivaling them.

Occasionally, when we veer from our lane and look too closely at those running next to us, we can become bossy and critical of them. This behavior will not lead you to success. It will only distract you from your goals. Keep your distance, and allow others to continue in their marked lanes. It is a recipe for disaster when some of us are in power and decide for others without knowing their calling. By the same token, never let somebody push you into a lane not intended for you.

There are a lot of things that will happen that you can't control, but you can control what you do when they occur. So that's what everyone strives to do: have a positive attitude, keep going forward, and put in a lot of effort.

There are remarkable examples in history. King Uzziah was ready to burn incense in 2 Chronicles 26, but it was not his obligation. It was the priests' obligation. Leprosy sprang out on his forehead as a result of his failure to stay in his lane. In another incident in 1 Samuel 13, when his men began to scatter and Samuel had yet to arrive, Saul made a burnt offering. When Samuel arrived and saw what Saul had done, he told him that, because Saul foolishly had not kept the command of God to wait for Samuel, his kingdom would not endure. Had he obeyed God's command, God would have established Saul's kingdom over Israel for all time.

When you stay in your lane, you will be successful. When you cross lanes, you will lose the race, even if it appears that you have won.

Many people may disagree with the stay-in-your-lane concept. Some may say that in order to be successful, you must step outside of your comfort zone and try something new. It's good to try something new, but keep it inside your comfort zone. There may be many things within you that are dormant and need to be activated. You must determine if those things are the races for which you were selected.

Questions for discussion

1. How would you describe the view from your lane?
2. Are you comfortable?
3. The example of Samuel shows what can happen when we stray from our lane and run out ahead of God. Have you ever done this? What was the result?
4. Sometimes it IS important to try new things. Write down two or three NEW things you can do to move ahead in business, life, and your spiritual walk?

"If you have no confidence in self, you are twice defeated in the race of life. With confidence, you have won even before you have started."

(Marcus Garvey)

Chapter 2

Live with Confidence!

The Second Ingredient for Success

Confidence is an ingredient that will allow you to achieve anything you desire. Once you have confidence, you are on your way to success. You may be suffering from low self-esteem, but over time, you may build your confidence and begin to change those self-defeating feelings with the aid of some encouraging points about confidence and the support of individuals in your inner circle.

Finding the appropriate tools to change your mentality can help you break the pattern of low self-confidence, regardless of its origin—whether you're feeling down on yourself because you don't make enough money, you are currently dealing with a poor body image, or something totally different.

It is most important to remember that you should not be afraid of anyone or anything. If you have faith, you will trust in the Lord, believe in yourself, and be fearless, strong, and courageous as you go confidently along your path. This is well said in Psalms 27:1.

> ***The Lord is my light and my salvation —whom shall I fear? The Lord is the stronghold of my life—of whom shall I be afraid?***

The Confident Life—The Key to Living with Confidence Is Positivity.

Always assume the best, be it in your business or your marriage. Even if it appears that you are failing, don't think of it as a failure.

There are times in our lives when we can't get what we want, and the reason is none other than a lack of confidence. Lack of confidence can be one of the biggest obstacles in life and spoil your ingredient for success. While some of us aren't frightened to venture out on our own, we frequently need the help of others. Although there is nothing wrong with asking for help, because no man is an island, there are still some things you can do on your own without asking for others' help. Frequently depending on others is a symptom of a basic lack of confidence.

On the other hand, some of us decide against seeking assistance because we think we shouldn't. We have an "I can't" mentality, which causes us to live in dread, only imagining the things we want in life.

Each time we truly confront our fear, we develop strength, courage, and confidence. We must do what we believe is impossible. Individuals resemble stained-glass windows. When the sun is out, they glitter and dazzle, but only inner light can bring out their full beauty when night falls. Your inner light is the true self-confidence that makes you unique in your own way.

So don't hold off until everything is perfect. Nothing will ever be ideal for us. There will always be difficulties, barriers, and unfavorable circumstances. Start right now. You will become more and more successful with every step you take, as well as more and more skilled, confident, and self-assured.

Trust God. Lacking faith in the Lord is one of the key reasons we don't live with confidence. Trusting in the Lord is one approach to growing in your faith. If you put your trust in the Lord, you'll realize that He is your strength, provider, and light. You shouldn't be terrified if you sincerely believe in the Lord. Believing in Him, you won't be afraid of anything or anyone, including your adversaries and failure.

Here are a few of the lessons I have learned through experience, and they have helped me live with confidence.

1. Don't let society's definition of success define you. Don't let your outward appearance consume you. Don't let your family history consume you. Avoid attempting to replicate someone else; just be you.

2. Believe in yourself. Have faith that you can fulfill your calling. Don't let other people's negative opinions about you influence you. Be aware of who you are. Be aware of your skills and the needs that you were called to fill. That being said, it's about time to arm yourself with all the information and resources you require to live a confident life.

3. Don't worry about anything if you want to live with confidence. There will be some setbacks and rejections, but don't let them worry you. Consider them chances. The Lord's word exhorts us not to worry about our lives. If you worry, you'll end up being fearful, which will lead to a lack of faith, which will lead to a lack of trust in the Lord and a lack of confidence in yourself. When you feel

yourself starting to worry, remind yourself that worrying won't fix anything. Being at peace is the greatest course of action since it allows you to live a confident life.

4. Remember, every day when you wake up to confront this chaotic world, God is with you, so just be brave and strong. Keep in mind that God is your shepherd. You can take risks if you are brave and powerful. Economics 101 taught me that the larger the risk, the greater the gain. Also, most of us have often heard the famous verse found in Joshua 1:9.

   Have I not commanded you? Be strong and courageous. Do not be afraid; do not be discouraged, for the Lord your God will be with you wherever you go.

5. Be positive. Positivity is the key to living with confidence. Don't launch a business anticipating failure. Always assume the best. Don't get married anticipating a failed union. Always assume the best. Even if it appears that you are failing, don't think of it as a failure. Take it as one more step of learning while moving toward your goals.

I will conclude this chapter with a verse from Psalms 27:3 for those who lack confidence in their lives.

> ***Though an army besiege me, my heart will not fear; though war break out against me, even then I will be confident.***

Questions for discussion

1. Would you say you are a confident person?
2. Do you struggle with self-esteem? Do you compare yourself to others?
3. How does your faith affect your confidence level when starting something new, perhaps a new business venture or relationship?
4. Positivity is key. What does walking into the day with a positive outlook look like to you? How does a negative mood affect your day?

Chapter 3

Be Honest!

The Third Ingredient for Success

We may occasionally be forced to pick between different things we enjoy because of our daily lives. The ideals we upheld as children, which have shaped who we are today, should never be compromised for this reason. Therefore, whatever happens in our lives shouldn't alter what already exists.

Sometimes a need for something is so strong that we don't even think twice about doing anything just to get it. We even agree to lower our standards or compromise our integrity, sometimes to the point of telling a lie or two.

I believe all of us at one point in our lives have told a lie. Sometimes it seems easier to tell a lie than to tell the truth, especially when you find yourself in a situation in which you think the only solution is to hide the truth. However, what we don't realize is that the truth is like a bright ray of light that can never be kept hidden; it will eventually come out. So it is best to always be honest, even if it means losing someone in a relationship or losing an opportunity for a major contract.

The Lord has always disliked lies and those who are fond of lying.

> ***The Lord detests lying lips, but He delights in people who are trustworthy.***
>
> **(Proverbs 12:22)**

Seeing so many people who seem successful, it is easy to assume that some of those triumphs may have resulted from dishonesty. Success based on deception is transient and will ultimately fail. Some people use dishonest practices to create vast empires. Some individuals enter into partnerships based on dishonest behavior. Some people commit theft and lie to achieve their goals. All such people must feel a ton of remorse, though, and probably worry about what will happen to them if they are discovered.

Oddly, most of the time, the individuals we lied to will remember that lie. Sometimes we lie so often that we forget what we lied about.

Anyone who doesn't take the truth seriously in small matters cannot be trusted in large ones, either.

(Albert Einstein)

With truth and honesty comes trust. Nobody will ever trust a person in any matter if there is even a slight bit of doubt about his honesty and integrity.

Why do most people lie? What makes them so intent on hiding the actual truth?

There are several reasons. We tell lies to win others over and gain acceptance. We lie because we are greedy and constantly want more. In our minds, lying serves as safety. Our lies will eventually catch up with us, which could cause humiliation, disgrace, and numerous losses.

Sadly, some of the individuals to whom we lied in order to impress them might not be there to stand by us when the truth comes out. Most likely, they will be in opposition to our lies, which will teach us a powerful lesson on why we should never lie under any circumstances.

There is another proverb that is related to dishonesty and how it eats away at everything we are trying to gather for ourselves and for our future.

> ***Dishonest money dwindles away, but whoever gathers money little by little makes it grow.***
>
> **(Proverbs 13:11)**

Earning anything in the name of dishonesty will never let you prosper, grow, and achieve success, be it in your relationship or your new career or job. The consequences of lying include death—not necessarily physically, but in terms of your marriage, a partnership, or perhaps your company.

Most of us must have heard about the tale of Ananias and Sapphira from the fifth chapter of Acts. Let us learn from their mistakes.

Acts 5 contains Ananias and Sapphira's tragic tale, which is very sad. The depiction of the early church in Jerusalem, a group of believers who were so moved by the Holy Spirit that they were of one thought and heart, actually begins at the end of chapter four. The apostles, who proclaimed and gave testimony of the risen Savior, were endowed with great power and grace. The people's hearts were so closely interwoven that they held all of their belongings lightly and freely shared them with one another, not out of coercion, but out of love. The apostles delivered the presents to those in need after receiving money from those who sold their land and homes.

Ananias and Sapphira, his wife, were two of the members of this group; they, too, sold a field. Holding back a portion of the proceeds from their sale,

Ananias distributed only a portion of the money to the apostles. He pretended, however, to have handed over all the money.

Others may have been duped by this fraudulent act, but Peter, who was filled with the power of the Holy Spirit, was not. Peter immediately saw that Ananias had deceived not just him, but also God, and he denounced him. Ananias collapsed and perished.

When Sapphira arrived, she, too, deceived both God and Peter by claiming that they had given the entire sum from the sale of the land to the church. She likewise collapsed and passed away at Peter's feet once her lie was discovered.

The lesson that needs to be learned from this story is clear. Once your lies are caught, your reputation and integrity will be shattered. It will be exceedingly difficult to win back people's trust. In fact, thereafter, some people will always call you a liar, no matter how hard you work to change your life. This is true even if it was just one small lie. By lying, you risk losing a lot since no one will want to help you in any matter once the lie has been revealed.

It is easy to see that there is some magic in truth, honesty, and openness about everything. It always feels as if a weight were lifted from your chest once you open up in front of your loved ones about everything. Honesty always gives you a chance to live freely, without care in the world.

Also, being truthful will help you win people over. You will prosper and advance in your career when people have confidence in you. People will warm up to you. People will support you, and your company will expand and prosper as soon as you have that support. Your honesty will be praised by the Lord. Being honest will help your marriage and family relationships flourish.

On the other hand, being dishonest never brings peace, and our actions keep us awake at night. Because we are living a lie, and hence are not living freely, we feel guilty and are not being genuine to ourselves.

In conclusion, under no circumstances should you jeopardize your integrity by being dishonest. No matter how minor it seems, always be sincere. Once you show that you are honest, you will succeed. Economic dealings or personal relationships with dishonest people is never desirable.

Questions for discussion

1. Are you an honest person? Have you ever told a lie for selfish gain?
2. How did you feel about the lie?
3. Have you ever had to hold your true feelings inside for fear of reprisal? How does that make you feel?
4. Being honest helps to make us authentic. Describe what it means to be authentic.

“Whoever heeds life-giving correction will be at home among the wise. Those who disregard discipline despise themselves, but the one who heeds correction gains understanding.”

(Proverbs 15:31–32)

Chapter 4

Be Receptive to Feedback and Constructive Criticism

The Fourth Ingredient for Success

This brief saying in the Bible is straightforward but meaningful. How well can you hear those who are correcting you?

Wisdom requires humble acceptance of criticism and guidance. If you dislike being corrected, you reject wisdom, which is essential for leading a fulfilling life. You must learn to take criticism if you want to be a successful person.

If you reject instruction and correction, which are essential for leading a wealthy and successful life, you have rejected the very tools of wisdom. Learning from others' criticism, instruction, rebukes, criticisms, and cautions is a valuable, fundamental life principle, and it can help you along the road to success.

Criticism occurs when someone disapproves of your behavior, activities, beliefs, etc.; when they correct you for making a mistake; or when they critique or forewarn you that your current course of action is unwise and will lead to suffering or trouble.

Accepting and appreciating criticism is challenging. Why? Because every person believes they are right, we dislike anyone who corrects and forewarns us about the foolishness of our decisions, traits, or behavior. However, if you are wise, you will question all of your beliefs and viewpoints.

What is criticism? It is guidance from someone who wants to assist you in living a prosperous life by trying to prevent you from hurting yourself in any number of ways. You must be willing to examine yourself in the light of criticism. Criticism or caution guides you in the right direction so that God might reward and favor you in your life. It is required for moral behavior.

Where does criticism come from? Initially, it starts with parents. In almost every way, parents are wiser than their children. While this gap narrows with experience, maturity, and age, it is so great in childhood and youth that parental reprimands must be regarded as divinely inspired knowledge.

Criticism in the form of positive feedback also comes from wise and experienced leaders, such as teachers, pastors, bosses, husbands, and other authorities. In order to demonstrate their love for you, they are required by God's commandment to correct any sin in your life.

Does love serve to validate it? Do you accept love in a correction? No, you do not. So reacting positively to constructive criticism is a moral test that you must pass if you want to succeed.

> ***Criticism may not be agreeable, but it is necessary. It fulfills the same function as pain in the human body. It calls attention to an unhealthy state of things.***
>
> **(Winston Churchill)**

Feedback and constructive criticism can be seen as negative or positive, depending on how it is given and received and who provided it. Some individuals deliberately and intentionally criticize others just to hurt them. However, you must be wise enough to distinguish good feedback from bad advice.

Overall, I think constructive criticism is a very important ingredient for success. Sometimes you are so preoccupied with your own thoughts and beliefs that you cannot see different perspectives. Perhaps you do not even trust anyone. Perhaps you think you know everything. But constructive criticism given with love will help you find something good and positive to soften the blow of the real critique being offered.

To truly accept criticism gracefully, examine its content, focusing on the message, not the messenger. In so doing, you may realize that the criticism allows you to grow and become successful.

Someone provided me with constructive feedback on the direction of *Financially Speaking*, a show I host every Tuesday. Initially, I was distraught, but as I reflected on what the gentleman said, I realized he had a valid point, and I had to refocus on the show's real purpose. Had the gentleman not contacted me, my show perhaps would not have improved and become more effective.

Many times we get defensive when receiving constructive criticism. Sometimes we get so upset that we discontinue speaking to the individual who provided the feedback. However, it is helpful to remember that accurate and constructive feedback can also come from flawed sources.

The best thing to do is not to react immediately. Digest and consider the feedback. Receiving well-intentioned criticism and implementing the recommended suggestions can make your life successful.

Constructive criticism should be seen as a measure of your performance. Lack of feedback can be detrimental to your success; you may think things are going well because there is no feedback, and then continue with the same pattern.

If you are on the receiving end of constructive criticism, don't throw it away. Insight from a trusted, objective source about your work, management style, or your actions is priceless. You want to keep it coming, and that means not reacting in a way that scares off the giver or makes them less willing to give you feedback in the future.

Imagine if you were on the job, but you were not given constructive feedback. You would think all is well when it isn't. And then if you left that job and got another one in which feedback is regularly given, you may take it personally and react negatively to the constructive criticism.

Some criticism can be very destructive and petty. You will have to learn to distinguish the difference, as there are many complainers out there too.

Accepting feedback and constructive criticism is a wise thing, and it will make you more successful at the end of the day. If you do not accept the criticism, someone else may take that criticism and run with it, and in the end become more successful than you. Do not become bitter with individuals who provide criticism; otherwise, your life will be full of bitterness and lack of trust, and you will live a defeated life.

Questions for discussion

1. Can you take criticism? Or does it make you defensive?
2. Discuss a time in your life when someone gave you constructive criticism? What was the result? Would you handle it differently?
3. How does criticism lead to success?
4. Have you ever criticized a coworker, business partner, or spouse? What is your approach to criticism?

“All roads that lead to success have to pass through hard-work boulevard at some point.”

(Eric Thomas)

Chapter 5

Work Hard

The Fifth Ingredient for Success

What is a common trait among all successful persons you have encountered in your personal or professional life? They all put in a lot of effort and don't let up until they have what they desire.

Some people believe they can talk themselves into and out of any circumstance without doing any work. Some relationships are built solely on verbal communication. Some people have exceptional communication skills, and they can persuade a partner to stay in a relationship merely by talking. Don't fall into the trap of only dreaming about success. It is easy to fantasize about wealth and success, but unless you are willing to get out there and work for it, dreams will always remain dreams. However, faith without action is useless.

There is no special formula. There are no quick fixes. There aren't any strategies. No tactics. No miraculous elixir. There is and always has been one requirement: hard work.

Hard Work

Hard work is important if you want to live a successful life, accomplish your goals, and feel wonderful about yourself. However, developing a strong work ethic requires persistence, motivation, tenacity, and determination.

Everyone needs a little dose of freshly brewed motivation from time to time to keep them focused on their objectives and on the road to success, regardless of whether they have just begun their first job or have been in their field for a while.

Sometimes talking works, but only temporarily, since you will ultimately talk yourself out of a job or a relationship because there won't be any proof that the talking worked. It is crucial that you stop idle chatter and put in hard effort in all areas of your life, including your profession, marriage, family, and even your spirituality.

> ***All hard work brings a profit, but mere talk leads only to poverty.***
>
> **(Proverbs 14:23)**

The idiom "Talk is cheap" is the contemporary equivalent of this proverb. Words are simple, but they seldom produce beneficial results until they are put into practice. In the end, one must work hard to achieve anything; action, not just rhetoric, is required. It's simple to talk about our goals all day long, but if all we do is talk, we won't go far. The idle talker just becomes impoverished, rather than being rewarded. Ultimately, success almost always comes to those who work for it.

All around us are multiple examples of people who have worked hard and succeeded.

God has equipped us with the skills, abilities, and gifts we need to succeed in every area of life. Multiple Bible verses about hard labor serve as simple reminders that the Lord is always there and at our side, even if it's often easy to forget that.

> ***Those who work their land will have abundant food, but those who chase fantasies have no sense.***
>
> **(Proverbs 12:11)**

In this passage, Solomon contrasts the importance of productive labor with the stupidity of idly passing the time. Wise farmers in Israel's agricultural civilization recognized the critical need to cultivate the soil at the proper time. The act of sowing and plowing was necessary for a harvest, which provided food for the table. However, a fool would waste his time engaging in fancies, such as looking for lost gold. It makes sense for a person to pursue a job in the contemporary world and take care of their house, family, and other things. Foolish individuals ignore those responsibilities in favor of focusing on inconsequential activities.

According to the Lord's word, effort results in gain. Too many of us are unmotivated and just plain lazy. Some of us think we naturally qualify for particular jobs and resources, without having to strive for them. But to gain certain privileges, you must work for them.

There are many rivalries in the business world. Therefore, you must put in a lot of effort to have a competitive advantage over your rivals. Entrepreneurs who are successful have worked hard to achieve their success. Usually, they've worked nonstop, not just from nine to five, to stay on top of the competition. Some new hires get promoted more quickly than long-term employees, and most of the time it's because they worked hard. Sadly, some workers waste a lot of time warming chairs and browsing the Internet; then they become irritated when those who were hired after them are given promotions.

And if it's about relationships, then whether you like it or not, relationships are competitive. To keep their marriages strong, husbands and wives must put forth a lot of effort. Some people, whether they're married or not, don't care; they seek out married individuals. Sometimes it really feels as if others can fill some gap you feel exists in your marriage, but that's not the case. They can never be a permanent presence in your life because that's not what their end goal is. Thus, if you want to continue a relationship with your spouse, despite all the arguments and differences, you need to put in a lot of effort and remain dedicated to you marriage; that is what is needed for your relationship to succeed. Relationships require effort and cannot be saved by love alone.

In today's busy world, it's easy to focus on saving your relationship with a person, while forgetting that your relationship with God also requires your efforts. No matter how mature you are, your relationship with God might still fall apart if you do not worship Him with dedication. There is a lot of temptation in life's chores and luxuries, and if you are not careful, you will fall into the enemy's trap so easily that your connection with your God will be lost forever. So put in great effort to preserve your spiritual connection to God. Keep your word, and follow His instructions.

In short, just be the best you can be. Working hard is one way to do that. Avoid choosing the simple path. You won't have to worry about working hard if you know what you want to do.

Working hard may occasionally be exhausting, isolating, and difficult. You may feel at times that, despite your efforts, nothing is happening. Be patient throughout this process, and keep in mind that everything has its time and season. Eventually, you will see your rewards.

I'm encouraging you to work hard in this chapter, but it's important that you cultivate strategies to also work efficiently so that you can maintain a healthy balance between your job and family—that should be the ultimate goal of everyone's life.

Questions for discussion

1. Are you willing to work hard?
2. Describe a time when hard work paid off for you.
3. How can you balance work and family?
4. The Bible says that God gives us the gifts—skills, abilities, and knowledge—to be successful. What do these three ingredients look like to you?

“Communication is key.”

Chapter 6

Communicate Effectively

The Sixth Ingredient for Success

How frequently have you heard the phrase "Communication is key"? We all communicate daily, whether through spoken words, written letters, or nonverbal cues. Why is it so crucial?

Communication is the act of passing knowledge from one person to another. However, it is important to realize that communication is only successful if the recipient comprehends the message.

Recently, I witnessed firsthand how even kids can become irritated if what they are trying to convey is not understood. Perhaps we should add to that statement that communication is only effective when the intended recipient understands the message.

From the moment we get up and turn on the radio, read the newspaper, drive by billboards on the way to work, and pay attention to train announcements, communication is all around us. Communication during the workday enables duties to be accomplished thoroughly, eventually elevating our, and the company's, professionalism.

Effective communication skills are highly prized in business. Leaders with poor communication skills are frequently to blame for problems with productivity.

In daily life, communication enables us to connect with people, share our experiences and needs, and strengthen our bonds. It allows us to communicate our views, share information, and express our emotions. All of us communicate, either effectively or ineffectively. We must know the difference between them and their pros and cons.

Effective communication is essential in both our personal and professional lives since ineffective communication can lead to both short- and long-term hostility, as well as lower productivity. While communicating, we frequently forget to consider the mechanics of how we communicate and receive information, but being more conscious of this may help resolve issues and enhance relationships.

Ineffective communication is one of the main causes of some of our failures. It occurs when we make assumptions, keep quiet about things, and fail to communicate exactly what has been done, what is necessary, and what is desired.

Too frequently, we assume that others are aware of our intentions. Even when we do not communicate at all, we sometimes expect a positive result. Despite having accomplished a lot, leaders have failed because of poor communication.

With the development of technology, it has become simple to communicate with everyone at once, particularly through social media. Everyone can receive the same message at the same time by having it delivered simultaneously to everyone.

However, the benefit of having everyone physically present is that if a message is not clear, everyone has the chance to ask for clarification. Family, business, and church meetings should be held regularly. There are a lot of rumors and misinformation out there, but when you come together in person, these can be dispelled.

The Jews of every nation heard their own language being spoken on the day of Pentecost, so they were able to hear the messages. However, it is important that messages are not simply heard; they must be understood. So we must effectively convey our messages to ensure that the recipient easily understands them.

Misunderstandings occur when our messages are not clearly understood by the recipients. This happens all too often when we communicate. Some messages are too complex for us to understand, so even though the intended audience hears them, they are not effectively communicated.

Keep your messages brief. Avoid excessive use of big words; you do not have to prove that you are well educated. You are not a good communicator if you use words and expressions that people do not understand—you might leave a lasting impression, but your message was not effectively conveyed.

Communicating effectively can allow you to win an election. It will make you a successful leader. It will eliminate misunderstandings, reduce confusion, and foster unity in the workforce, the church, the country, and the home.

Each person in a relationship has unique communication needs and preferences. Finding a communication strategy that works effectively is essential to the relationship's success. This requires effort and hard work.

When speaking with your partner, be clear so that your point of view is received and understood. After your partner has spoken, confirm what you heard to verify that you understood what they were trying to convey.

In conclusion, never take it for granted that you have been understood. Communicate effectively, even if it involves using social media. Encourage feedback to ensure that the message has been properly communicated.

Questions for discussion

1. Do you consider yourself a good communicator? Why or why not?
2. Have you ever been misunderstood? How did it make you feel?
3. Jesus often used parables to communicate his message. Personal stories or anecdotes can be quite impactful. Can you think of a good story about your own life that will illustrate an important point?
4. Misunderstandings can lead to failure. Has this ever happened to you?

> *"Where there is no vision, the people perish..."*

(Proverbs 29:18, King James Version)

Chapter 7

Plainly Write Down the Vision

The Seventh Ingredient for Success

Why is it necessary to write down your objectives? It may sound cliché, but there is a correlation between writing down your goals and achieving them.

It has something to do with how our minds work. When you write something down, you use both sides of your brain: the imaginative right and the logic-based left hemispheres. This is well-known in the business sphere, particularly among CEOs who utilize this principle to keep on track with their numerous obligations.

Certain times of the year and seasons in our lives may motivate us to formulate our objectives. But often we can't seem to get to it.

Goal Setting

I've discovered goal setting has several stages. A notion comes to mind, and we start thinking about doing something. For a while, we fantasize about how we will feel once we have achieved that particular goal. We usually stick our key in the ignition a few times, but never work up the nerve to put the car in Drive because we don't yet know the direction we need to go. This is what we do wrong. We should always formally set our goals and map out our strategy before starting to work on achieving them.

I believe we all have desires, yet some of us do nothing about them. In truth, some of us die without ever pursuing our dreams. Writing down and making clear your vision is an important step toward achieving your goals. Place those written objectives in a visible location, someplace you will see them frequently; this will serve as a continual reminder and, perhaps, will push you to the point of implementing your plan of action.

There are several scriptures related to goal setting in the Bible. One of them is:

Write down the revelation and make it plain on tablets so that a herald may run with it.

(Habakkuk 2:2, New International Version)

The same command is given by God in Isaiah, Jeremiah, and Revelation.

From the above scripture, we can clearly learn a few things that God wants to tell us for our daily lives:

- It is important to physically write things down. This creates a record of crucial events and serves as a road map for the journey ahead.
- This written account will capture your long-term goals and provide a plan of action so that common blunders are avoided.

We know that the Bible is God's unadulterated word. We receive it as if it were a collection of wonderful letters from our Father. We revere it as our life's manual. That is Bible-based Christianity. But do you understand that without a series of people saying yes to writing the Word down, we wouldn't today have that guidebook, the Bible?

Similarly, God desires to collaborate with you to see incredible things happen in your life. It begins by seeking Him out, becoming silent, and listening.

In my own life, I've noticed that my wife has her visions written out and posted in the bathroom. Of course, we use the bathroom every day, and so we see those goals every single day. At the end of her list of goals, she posted the scripture:

> *"I can do all this through Him who gives me strength."*
>
> (Philippians 4:13)

This is a reminder that her visions are achievable, especially if given by God. Our church's vision and mission statements are visibly displayed in the foyer, so you see them as you enter our home.

Vision

What is a vision? It is the foreseeing of where you want to go in life and what you want to accomplish. Your goals serve as a road map for your vision. You cannot create a road map unless you have a clear picture of where you want to go. Defining a vision is the most successful goal-setting method since it provides your goals a sense of direction.

Visioning is one of the most effective strategies I've seen in action. It assists many individuals and organizations in achieving their goals. People become more creative and imaginative when they broaden their thoughts and examine their aims from a new angle. Visioning can be described as the creation of a desired road map of your future. Visioning is unique. It is determined and unmistakably tenacious. Visioning evaluates and delineates present practice to improve it and to achieve qualitative results.

After settling on a vision, the next important step is writing it down. Many of us wake up each morning without a plan in place for our lives. It is like hopping in your car and driving with no known destination. However, I believe when most of us get in a car, we have an idea of where we are going, whether it is to work, church, school, or home. Unfortunately, with no written plan, we do not know what to do when we get to our destination.

Write your vision down on a large piece of paper. Tick off each point as you achieve it.

Some of you may question why you should write anything down if you have everything in your head. The act of writing your life plan down, and the list that will result from that, will remind you, your family, and your employees of the tasks ahead. It also serves as motivation.

Furthermore, it is easy to forget. So a written document is a great way to communicate and share your goals with the relevant individuals who can assist you in staying on track to achieve your vision.

First, we visualized. Then, we wrote it down. That brings us to the third important point, according to Bible. We must plainly state our vision, which is foreseeing where you want to go and what you want to accomplish.

There is no right or wrong when it comes to your vision. Your vision is your vision. However, your written vision must be easily understood. The simplest thing to do is make a bucket list of your life goals. Under each item, write down the steps and timeline necessary for achieving that vision.

Achieving your vision will require patience and faith; it may take a while. However, do not give up; if your vision comes from God, you can achieve it.

> ***For the revelation awaits an appointed time; it speaks of the end and will not prove false. Though it lingers, wait for it; it will certainly come and will not delay.***
>
> **(Habakkuk 2:3)**

We are all striving for greater results. Writing out your goals is a wonderful place to start. It's a simple approach that reduces stress and allows you to be more efficient. It's time to give it a shot and make the most of your opportunities.

Some of you may be wondering what a written vision has to do with success. It has a great deal to do with success. It's similar to utilizing a GPS tracker to acquire directions to your location. Without a GPS tracker, you may become disoriented and not know where you are heading. Your vision may appear to be unattainable, but with faith you can realize it. Recording your vision provides a wonderful measuring instrument for your success.

Finally, the Lord's word declares that, without vision, we perish. This phrase alone demonstrates the importance of vision in achieving success.

Of course, writing down a vision is not enough. Once your vision is written, do something with it. Implement it and take action.

Questions for discussion

1. Write down your goals for the next several days, weeks, months, and years.
2. How do those goals differ from your vision?
3. What can you do right now to start working toward your long-range goals?
4. Make a vision board. Keep it in a place where you will see it every day.

Chapter 8

Choose the Right Team!

The Eighth Ingredient for Success

The right team is the eighth key to success in life. Just as a husband and wife need to be on the same team for their marriage to be successful, having the right team in place is crucial to the effectiveness and success of any workplace, whether it be a company, a school, or a football team. The potential to succeed is even greater with the right people on board.

The first step in creating a solid and long-lasting business is always assembling the right team. Your team's strength—not the quality of your concept or the quality of your final product—determines whether you succeed or fail.

Team Building

Finding a group of individuals with the ideal combination of professional skills is only one aspect of creating a successful team. No matter what industry you are in, what kind of business you have, or where in the world you are, you need to assemble the best team possible if you want to succeed.

Finding individuals who will greatly benefit the team is a difficult task. This has to do with selecting people who have the same values, vision, and goals as you, individuals who are capable of handling current and future tasks and responsibilities, those who are driven to succeed, who complement the other team members, and who are quick to pick up new skills.

Each of us needs to look for a variety of distinctive traits that reveal people who can contribute to the team and get along with others. Finding the right blend of skills and talent is a difficult task because even the most talented individuals may not function well in a team. Nevertheless, it is crucial.

> ***Jesus went up on a mountainside and called to him those he wanted, and they came to him. He appointed twelve that they might be with him***

> ***and that he might send them out to preach.***
>
> **(Mark 3:13–14)**

Jesus found it difficult to get away from the crowd, but He needed some seclusion. He had spent the night before alone in prayer to God. He only selected those who would be His closest followers after consulting with His Father. He has already picked Simon and Andrew (Mark 1:16–17), James and John (Mark 1:19–20), and Levi (Mark 2:13–14). He completed the number of His inner circle, or "the twelve," as Mark refers to them.

The mountain referred to is most likely one of the hills around Capernaum. The village is 600 feet below sea level. The ground climbs sharply and reaches 236 feet within a few miles. That's not a particularly high height, but it's still an increase of more than 800 feet.

When Jesus calls these men, He does not mean for them to simply quit their employment or leave their homes, which are great sacrifices in and of themselves. Jesus commands people to follow Him with both their minds and their spirits. These are men who appear to be interested in His work beyond healing. Their hearts are receptive to His instruction.

This is the mentality we should adopt. Our entire selves—our brains, hearts, time, effort, and priorities—should be put into our response when Jesus asks us to follow Him. Additionally, we ought to be prepared to give up our friendships (Luke 14:26), material goods (Mark 10:21), reputations (Philippians 3:3–11), and even our lives if necessary (Philippians 2:17).

But the twelve are only getting started. They have no idea that ten of them will be martyred for Jesus and an eleventh will be deported. They only know that they must say yes right then. They will allow Jesus to transform their hearts during the ensuing years and discover that the price was worth it (1 Corinthians 2:9). God affirms that He can work in such ways with us as well (Philippians 2:13).

Even Jesus Christ had a support team. Jesus chose twelve apostles to be His inner circle, and the people He chose came from a variety of backgrounds; His chosen would be utilized to restore the Kingdom.

But you've heard the story about how one of His team members betrayed Him. Of course, since the prophecy had to be fulfilled, Jesus was aware that this betrayal would occur.

There are numerous Judases in your home, church, and workplace. Take note of this. Select the correct folks who will help you to achieve your goals.

One of the first things to do is to seek the Lord in prayer, asking for direction in choosing the right person or persons for your company. Sometimes we are so desperate for someone, whether it be a husband, a wife, a girlfriend, a boyfriend, or an employee, that we select the first person who comes along. Because of our hasty decision, we end up with the wrong person.

After you pray, be patient. God will send the right person or persons. In Luke 6:12, Jesus prayed to God all night, and the next day He appointed his twelve apostles.

To be successful, you must surround yourself with people who will help you succeed. When Jesus designated the twelve, He immediately sent them out on a mission to preach the message, heal the sick, and cast out demons. He had faith in their competence and independence; He knew they would complete their tasks.

Your team members should not be parasites. They should be able to assist you in achieving your goals. A husband and wife should complement and enhance one another. Employees should add value to your company. People should not be on your team because of their physical traits, empathy, or familiarity. Make certain they are wise and knowledgeable. Some people might not have much experience, but if they are willing to learn and have the appropriate attitude, you should hire and train them so they can benefit your business.

Each individual is a crucial piece of the puzzle that is the overall enterprise. Understand your position, as well as the duties of others. Make sure you take the time to grasp your job in the team, as well as the roles of your teammates. Ask questions until you have a thorough understanding of both your own and others' responsibilities, as well as how you may best support the team's success. Furthermore, if you understand your function and the duties of others, you will be able to interact with them more effectively.

This collaboration is more than just a kind gesture on your part. It is critical to the project's overall success. Look for opportunities and be open to collaborating.

The team's job, if completed successfully and efficiently, will result in enhancement. If both the husband and woman put effort into the marriage, the union is improved. Similarly, instead of leaving everything up to the leader, teams that put in a lot of effort, with each member doing their share of the work, will be more successful.

Working hard necessitates a lot of practice. If you are having fun, you will work hard. If you dislike the work involved in being a part of a team, do not join it.

You can also help the team by asking questions and connecting with other members. Don't be afraid to inquire. Questioning and providing updates are both forms of communication. Keep in touch with people. Timetables must be coordinated with everyone, not just the leader. Check in with other people. Collect their feedback. Determine completion benchmarks. Keep everyone updated on your progress. Communicate!

Seek the knowledge you gained from earlier duties and initiatives, whether small or enormous, and use it to improve your current outcome. Even though the aims were probably entirely different, you likely learned lessons that can be applied to your current situation—things you did well you can repeat, and things you could have done better you can correct on this project.

Jesus instructed His followers to carry out His wishes without payment and to refrain from carrying particular items. Today, too many people are doing things outside of their marriages or work, trying to make bargains or shortchange their spouse or company. Your spouse has wants; don't ignore them by playing games with them. Your employer's client is paying for services and has requirements.

You are compensated for your efforts. Stop attempting to strike side deals. Spending time on your phone or engaging in other nonbusiness activities will cause you to shortchange your clients' time. The customer should receive value for the money he spends. The client shouldn't be charged for your downtime.

Your team should be dedicated to you. A company can only be as good as its personnel. If you want to succeed, make sure your employees are on the same page and are eager to advance with you. A highly devoted workforce will stick by your company through ups and downs and devote themselves to its overall success. Anyone who "does not take up their cross and follow" is unworthy, Jesus said to His disciples in Matthew 10:38.

Too many marriages end in divorce because one of the partners decides to cheat on the other. Too many employees are dissatisfied with their jobs. They are starting their own businesses on the side in order to draw business away from their current company, both directly and indirectly. You, like Jesus's disciples, do not deserve to be a part of an organization if you are not dedicated and committed to it.

Your employees become dedicated to you and your organization, but it will take time and work. Begin by simply being human. It may sound strange, but it can be as simple as treating others as fellow human beings with feelings that matter. Listen to them and pay attention to little details, such as their children's names and personal events. Then recall them. It demonstrates that you care, and people frequently appreciate and remain loyal to you as a result.

Second, loyalty is developed over time via honesty and compassion for other people's points of view and ideas. It is critical in the workplace to offer everyone an equal opportunity to share their thoughts and concerns. In my experience, being fair and proactive with people has allowed for the development of profound trust in a relatively short period of time. Put yourself in the shoes of others at all times.

Loyalty is hard to earn and easy to lose. You must maintain consistency and fairness. I have come near to violating that trust by not expressing the reason for my actions.

Many leaders believe they are entitled to their team's trust and devotion; however, this is contrary to nature. No one is worthless. Deal with everyone fairly and with the same kindness you reserve for those in your inner circle—you know, the type of care and trust you show without expecting anything in return. Of course, you'll need to tailor this to your specific scenario.

When it comes to marriage, loyalty is choosing to love your spouse every day. It is impossible to accidentally fall in love with someone. Those who argue they are not responsible for another person's feelings are merely denying that they allowed those feelings to develop. Without thinking about how the other person may feel later, they decided to shatter their partner's heart.

It is about remaining strong and faithful in the face of difficulties in your relationship. It's about refusing to give up on your love and the person you adore; it's about battling and holding on until your dying breath.

Never abandon your companion in difficult times. Face the challenges together and remain loyal to one another by being each other's strength; you are a team.

Making your relationship a top priority is also a sign of loyalty toward your mate. Yes, there are other aspects of your life that require your attention, such as work and family, so you must learn how to strike the correct balance so that you do not feel stressed and burned out. A person who truly loves you will understand if they aren't at the top of your list for a time because he or she understands that in order to be the ideal partner, he or she must first be the best version of himself or herself.

It is critical to acknowledge the benefits of loyalty in maintaining your friendships, no matter how many problems you both endure. Although it is easier said than done, being honest and true to your partner is feasible if you trust in your love for each other.

Finding the ideal team is difficult. Sometimes you believe you know someone, just to discover later that the person you thought you knew is not who you thought they were. Don't be in a hurry to find the appropriate individuals. Before deciding to marry, you should date as much as possible. In business, enforce the probationary period, even if it means extending it, to ensure that you have the correct team before making a long-term commitment.

Finally, nothing should be taken for granted. Conduct reference checks on your team before engaging with them. You might be shocked by what you find. With the proper team, leaders will be able to accomplish their tasks in less time and spend more time with their families and friends.

Every great company is supported by an equally successful staff. Establishing and nurturing a team is the most critical stage of laying a strong foundation that can drive your business to success.

Questions for discussion

1. Are you a team player?
2. What does that mean?
3. If you are a team leader, what can you do to nurture and grow your team?
4. Are you a lone wolf? How does that affect your work?

“Therefore, I tell you, whatever you ask for in prayer, believe that you have received it, and it will be yours.”

Chapter 9

Belief!

The Ninth Ingredient for Success

Belief is the ninth component in my success formula. Whatever you ask for in prayer, believe that you will receive it, and it will be yours. Have faith that your marriage will work out. Never enter into a marriage with the expectation that it will fail; if you do, your belief will cause it to do so. Have faith that your job or business will succeed.

When you have faith in something or someone, you will go above and beyond to ensure success. You will occasionally face challenges that could put your views to the test. When you do, focus on your goals and see past any obstacles. Have faith in God. Recognize that He didn't bring you this far to let you down. Believe in yourself because when you do, you can be sure that you will succeed.

You weren't created to fail, after all. You were made for a reason, and that reason will enable you to succeed. You should believe in God since He created you, and He created you for a purpose. Believe also that He has a purpose in life for you. We place far too much faith in men, so when they let us down, we are hurt and disappointed. God, however, will never let us down. Many people, including non-Christians, are successful because of their faith.

Being unsuccessful at anything is very different from being a failure. The enemy wants us to think we are failures, but God doesn't see us that way. Even the challenging circumstances in life, those that don't turn out the way we hope or expect, will work out for our benefit. We are still developing as His children. But at the core of it all, we are His children, made in His likeness. And until the day we go from this Earth, He will keep forming and sculpting us to become more like Him.

You are the source of your own vision. If you share your vision with others, they might dissuade you. Even worse, someone else might try to take your idea and run with it. While sharing your vision with others is beneficial, you do not require their approval. You must have faith in your goals. How do you expect others to join you in ensuring that the vision is realized if you don't believe in it?

I think the core of Napoleon Hill's famous saying, "Whatever the mind can conceive and believe, it can achieve," is about visioning. The more clearly we can define our goals, whether they be corporate or personal, the more successful we will be. It takes effort to develop a vision. The process is challenging; it can require years of work and is definitely not a one-shot deal. Listen to others, to your instincts, and to a variety of possibilities as you distill an effective vision. It takes courage to create a vision, but anyone who is dedicated enough can do it.

It is quite difficult to believe in yourself when you repeatedly fail at something that other people perceive as being simple. When you lack confidence, you frequently concentrate on, and are more aware of, your limitations. They are painfully drawn to your attention as symbols of failure, weakness, and shame. It doesn't take long for "I'm horrible at this" to turn into "I'll never be excellent at anything!"

Everyone has both strengths and shortcomings. That's good news. In order to maximize the use of your strengths, you must learn how to recognize them. Stop wasting time on things for which you aren't wired. Identify your strengths, and put your efforts into getting better at those things if you want to start developing your confidence immediately.

Successful people focus on the positive—what they excel at—and assign what they're weak at to others, rather than fretting about falling short.

You will naturally feel more competent and confident when you change your focus to enhancing your abilities. And you can become a badass if you work hard to enhance your innate talents.

Perhaps you are not aware of some of your assets. To obtain some inspiration, consider the following statements and apply them to you: "Always has a broad-picture perspective," "Is a big-picture thinker," "Notices the little things," "Is detail-oriented," "Loves learning and studying," "Is a good communicator," "Never gives up," "Is hands-on," and "Is action-oriented."

Tell your loved ones, close friends, and coworkers about your strengths. What are some of the things they ask you for assistance with? Even though this activity may give you a confidence boost, you are not looking for compliments.

Knowing your strengths will enable you to concentrate more of your efforts on the areas in which you currently excel. You can develop in the directions you're naturally drawn. You can find the resources to handle anything once you are operating from a position of strength and confidence in your skills. You can quit hitting your head against a wall once you are aware of your natural abilities and limitations. Then you can focus on what you do best and discover solutions for tasks requiring expertise in which you are limited.

I recall the name change from Cable and Wireless to LIME at the business where I formerly worked. It was announced at a meeting of the company CEOs in the Cayman Islands, and then we all returned to our offices to tell the workers about it. It was challenging since I wasn't on board with the vision, and when I gave the presentation, one of my colleagues remarked that neither had I convinced him about the merits of the new vision, nor had I myself looked convinced.

You won't believe someone who is supporting you from the sidelines if you don't believe in yourself. Because of this, superb small-business coaches guide their clients toward success by nurturing talent, rather than providing encouragement.

According to Gallup's research, managers who give their staff members autonomy produce excellent results. Managers who concentrate on talent development achieve great results. Great coaches and managers inspire others by providing them with the tools, knowledge, and resources they need to be successful. To make people feel comfortable and bring out the best in everyone, they communicate with people utilizing techniques like conversational intelligence. Goal setting, performance evaluations, and positive thinking don't produce results on their own. None of those things is a solution if you don't think you have what it takes.

You must have confidence in yourself. You must have confidence in your ability to do the task, in spite of your flaws or deficiencies. Even if your family is not wealthy or you have a shameful history, you must have faith in yourself, faith that you can overcome your past and that you have a bright future. You must have faith that you can accomplish your goals and that Christ, who gives you strength, will enable you to do so.

Having confidence in your own abilities is what it means to believe in yourself. It entails having confidence in your capacity to accomplish goals. When you have confidence in yourself, you can overcome self-doubt and have the courage to act and complete tasks.

Success seems elusive when you're wallowing in anxieties, doubts, and self-destructive habits; no amount of knowledge, experience, or resources can make a difference in your life. Believe that you can achieve everything you set out to do. Believe …because you are what you think.

While having doubts occasionally is normal, you should never allow those doubts to rule your life. When you see that you are going to doubt something, stop, reprimand yourself, and replace your doubts with trust. You are capable of anything…as long as you believe in yourself.

What dream or belief did you abandon out of fear or lack of confidence? We've all been there. But you're going to stay there forever if you don't take care.

It is quite easy to believe in yourself. You, too, can succeed. Just keep in mind that belief is a tool. That notion is not at all novel. It has existed for many centuries; it has just been stated differently by different people. Express this idea in any way you wish, but the concept is the same.

Do you know what happened when I started using belief as a tool? I found that everything I formerly believed is true. And now I know that the other things that I think will one day be proven to be true.

You can accomplish anything your mind can imagine. Stop telling yourself you can't. Have faith and believe that you can.

Questions for discussion

1. Do you believe in yourself?
2. Have you ever had to stand your ground because of your beliefs? What was the result?
3. It's okay to believe in yourself even when others are critical. How does cri ticism affect belief?
4. Describe self-doubt. How can you change doubt into belief?

Chapter 10

We Need Money!

Tenth and Final Ingredient for Success

Money is never far away when it comes to success.

Money is important whether you are looking for love and happiness, freedom and time, a career and status, or a car, watch, and luxury. It gives us stability, security, liberty, and opportunity.

I don't believe success can be purchased. Success, in my opinion, is a sensation that comes from being genuinely pleased, appreciated, and fulfilled.

I'm sure you've heard the expressions "Money can't buy happiness," or "Some of the wealthiest individuals are unhappy," both of which are true to some extent. If they don't manage needs and every element of their lives—health, love, connection, and purpose, for example—happiness (success) will elude them, no matter how much money they have.

Money, on the other hand, is fairly vital as a resource, tool, energy, and currency to attain many of the things we strive to have and be. Even to fulfill your basic requirements—such as security or hunger, big house or little—you need money.

Money Equals Success?

We usually remark, "We don't need money to be successful," because money has been demonized as a result of all of the issues it creates. To satisfy your needs, you don't need to be a millionaire, or even have that much money, but you do need some.

The truth is that we require money to be successful in most situations. Financial considerations are one of the leading causes of divorce. Businesses are collapsing due to lack of funds and, of course, poor financial management. Many individuals have ambitions and visions, but they lack the financial resources to put them into action. Some people want to advance their careers or objectives by seeking postsecondary education, but they lack the financial resources to attend college or university.

We live in a time in which the expense of living is constantly rising. We require funds in order to live comfortably in an apartment or house. The weather is so odd these days that we need to have the air conditioner on most of the time, but we need money to pay the power bill when it comes due. We must eat and live healthily, and we must have the money to do so. In short, we require money in order to live a prosperous life.

Of course, certain things cannot be purchased with money. It will not get you into paradise. It is not capable of curing incurable disorders. It cannot purchase true affection. It cannot buy you happiness.

Money is not everything, but it is quite significant. Money helps us reach our life goals and supports the things we care about the most: family, education, health care, charity, adventure, and pleasure. It enables us to obtain some of life's intangibles, such as freedom or independence; it offers the opportunity to maximize our abilities and talents. Money allows us to chart our own path in life, and it give us financial security. With money, much good can be done and much suffering can be avoided or eliminated.

However, money has its own constraints. It can provide us with the leisure to appreciate the little things in life more fully, but not the spirit of innocence and wonder that is required to do so. Money can buy us time to cultivate our strengths and talents, but it cannot buy us the guts and discipline to do so. Money can provide us with the ability to make a difference in the lives of others, but it cannot provide us with the motivation to do so. It can provide us with the time to create and nourish our relationships, but not the love and care that is required to do so. It has the potential to make us jaded, escapist, selfish, and lonely.

How much do you require? How much would it cost you to obtain it? Keeping these two issues in mind offers us a clear picture of money's link to happiness. We can never be satisfied if we have less than we need or if what we have is too expensive. We require money in order to eat, sleep, dress, work, play, relate, heal, move about, and enjoy creature pleasures. When selecting our style, we should keep in mind that it has a cost.

Evidence of the rich and famous's psychological and spiritual poverty abounds in our newspapers, magazines, tabloids, and television shows, and it hardly needs to be repeated here.

"We often think that if we just had a little bit more money, we'd be happier," says Catherine Sanderson, an Amherst College psychology professor, "but when we get there, we're not."

"Once basic human needs are addressed, a lot more money doesn't generate a lot more happiness," says Dan Gilbert, a Harvard University psychology professor and author of the new book *Stumbling on Happiness.*

Yes, we get a rush from pricey items at first. But we quickly grow accustomed to them. Economists refer to this state of running in place as the hedonic treadmill. The issue isn't money; we are the issue.

Money can help us find more happiness as long as we know what to anticipate from it. Many studies imply that shopping for a happy life is a costly exercise in futility. Money can bring us happiness, but only if we spend it wisely.

The question is not how much money anything costs, but how much money costs us. Money should not be allowed to cost us our souls, relationships, dignity, health, intelligence, or joy in the little things in life. People who identify their true beliefs and then align their money with those principles enjoy the greatest sense of financial and personal well-being.

What if we changed our negative perception of money as a source of greed and unhappiness to a positive impression that money can foster positive-energy exchanges and dream enablement? Would we have a better connection with it? Might that help eliminate the labels Evil or Dirty? Could it reduce jealousy caused by comparing financial wealth? Could it eliminate the anxiety of charging our worth? Could it also eliminate the desire for material things?

It may be radial thinking, but picture thinking of money as a type of LOVE.

I adore money, the opportunities and possibilities it provides, the adventures it allows, and the wonderful impact it can have on the world when utilized to exemplify our principles.

The capacity to keep, balance, and grasp what the cash or asset purchased signifies to you, for example, is the secret to my success and money.

- Luxury vacation = Long-lasting memories
- Large home full of laughter = Happiness
- Ability to assist others = Dedication

I recognize that this is a highly idealistic vision of the world, and I recognize that there are many very solid reasons to despise money, but I want you to examine it objectively and consider whether you may better embrace your relationship with money and attract greater success into your life.

Many people used to believe that being successful with money meant being wealthy. People were thought to be wealthy if they had a certain work title, lived in a huge house, drove costly cars, took frequent and luxurious vacations, and wore designer clothes.

That restricted and limited way of thinking is, thankfully, evolving. In recent years, there has been a greater focus on what it means to be wealthy. While a large house, costly automobiles, and other material possessions can be a sign of affluence—or debt!—they no longer command the same amount of admiration and envy as they once did.

These days, wealth is defined less by the number of zeros in your bank account, and more by having or earning enough to live on without the continual burden of money worries. It is being thankful for what you have. It means having enough freedom of choice to live your life on your own terms.

It is a sense of security to know that you earn enough to easily pay your mortgage. It is the ability to sleep easily, knowing that you have an emergency fund in place to cover any financial shocks, such as a recession, job loss, or unforeseen home or car repairs. It's the feeling of abundance, knowing you can treat your family to a beautiful dinner or a holiday if you choose. It's being in a place just because you want to, not because you feel obligated to show off your wealth.

It is the sense of accomplishment we feel when we make an investment that we understand and believe in, and the sense of accomplishment and exhilaration as we watch our investment grow.

> ***A feast is made for laughter, wine makes life merry, and money is the answer for everything.***
>
> **(Ecclesiastes 10:19)**

I understand that there are many interpretations of the scripture that says money is the answer to everything. It suggests that money protects you from the problems that come with being poor.

In a material sense, money can purchase almost anything. It elicits a response in everything, yet there are some things that are more valuable. Money cannot add years to your life, yet behaving wisely can protect life now and even open the door to eternal life.

Many people believe that you don't need money to be successful. Perhaps there are some legitimate grounds for such a remark, but I personally believe that money is required for success. Of course, what success means to you may not be the same thing I believe. As a result, many people believe that success should not be measured by how much money you have. That is correct. However, in order to arrive at your definition of success, you must first acquire funds. Let us not pretend that we do not require money to be successful.

Financial success allows us to have more freedom, choice, and security. It is feeling so confident in your own choices, prosperity, and financial security that you are pleased for the Joneses and everything they have—yet have no need to compare or compete with them.

Many people are surprised to learn that you don't need a lot of money to accomplish this. I work with families who make what others believe to be a subpar wage. Despite this, they are more abundant, feel wealthier, and live more freely than other families who make several times as much.

What is the distinction between them? It could be a combination of circumstances, but their financial mindsets play a significant impact.

Of course, there are those who have money but have failed marriages, failed relationships, failed enterprises, and failed jobs. Maybe it's because they're in the wrong relationship, maybe they're in the wrong business, or maybe they're in the wrong career. You must be in a relationship, business, or career that you are enthusiastic about. However, you will need money to preserve your relationship, money to build your business, and money to further your career.

While there will be arguments for and against whether or not you need money to be successful, we should never allow ourselves to become obsessed with our desire for money to the point that we become greedy for the love of money, which is, of course, the root of all evil.

Money is energy. It is a tool that we require to live our lives. In the same way that our bodies require food, we require money to go about our daily lives.

It does not reflect who we are or what we are worth as humans. It does not make one person better or more deserving than another.

Our sentiments about what we have will define our perception of prosperity. Success does not have to be measured by how much money we have, but we do require money to live successful lives. In my experience, the more content we are with what we have, the more we attract and the faster our wealth grows.

Questions for discussion

1. How would you describe your relationship with money?
2. Do you believe money can buy happiness? Why or why not?
3. Do you consider yourself to be smart with money, or is it an area in which you struggle? What steps can you take to improve your money matters?
4. Describe prosperity. Is it always about money?

Conclusion

Success in life is dependent upon how you define it. Maybe you're trying to figure out how to succeed so that you may have a flexible schedule or financial freedom.

Others may only wish to pursue their passions, while some may desire to explore the world.

Being successful can also be about achieving personal fulfillment; it's not always about being wealthy or receiving accolades.

What would your ideal day be like if you had to design it?

Would you be writing your book while lounging on Gracebay Beach in the Turks and Caicos Islands?

Do you envision yourself ascending Mount Kilimanjaro and taking that exhalation once you reach the summit? Or perhaps all you want to do is play with your kids all day?

It will be specific to you as to why you want to learn how to succeed in life. Success may mean different things to your partner, parents, and friends. However, their explanations do not apply to you.

While learning the art of success, you should concentrate on whatever it is that will make you feel content and joyful. Because we all want to feel important, most people worry about how to succeed.

Without any success, we can look back on our lives and be disillusioned by how little of an influence we had. We strive to survive and grow because we want to fulfill a higher mission.

Even if you don't achieve global success, others may still be impacted by your life. The desire to succeed will motivate you to overcome challenges, put in a little more effort, and pursue happiness, which will help you lead a more fulfilling life.

Learning how to succeed is now simpler than ever. Pay attention to the biblical references and steps in this book that required to succeed. Reaching your objective will turn into a new adventure every day if you let yourself celebrate tiny triumphs along the way, and you'll be more likely to stay on course. The knowledge you gain from doing this will help you develop yourself by exposing you to new and intriguing topics as you go.

Positivity is the one mandated principle that everyone must uphold at all times. Confidence in oneself and one's capacity for success are the cornerstones of cultivating a positive outlook. To keep trying despite obstacles in your path, it's critical to swap out any negative thoughts for optimistic ones.

You're likely to pick up new skills and develop new ways of thinking as you move toward achievement. Your objectives won't be achieved immediately. It is crucial to have a positive attitude throughout the process because it will require practice and dedication to obtain.

You may encounter days or situations along the way that require you to alter your perspective in order to improve a trying circumstance. When you're having a bad day or a bad week, pretend that you're having a good day or a good week.

Allow yourself the time and space to reflect on your situation while only using positive language, and then see how dramatically your day or week changes. Your entire life might change if you carry on in this manner for a very long period.

But if you discover that your objective has stalled in any way, you may need to be very honest with yourself about the reason why. Once you've come to a realization, try to find a means to inspire yourself to succeed.

Set a goal to push yourself beyond your comfort zone. This could include doing an extra set of squats, approaching your boss for a promotion, or even registering for a difficult college course you hadn't thought about before.

List the activities and people in your life that occupy your time or distract you. This may be a person who makes you anxious, a television program, or even a phone. When you need to concentrate on your goal, turn off your phone and place it in a separate room.

Put the remote across the room and switch off the television. Only stay in touch with those who have a positive influence on your life. The greatest time to start modifying your behaviors is right now so that you can avoid distractions and concentrate solely on obtaining achievement.

You can't rely on other people to accomplish your goals for you. A class cannot be taken for you by your best friend. Your mum won't be able to get you a raise. Your partner cannot lose extra weight for you. These are all things you must do on your own.

It can be beneficial to rely on others for emotional support, but just as you have your needs, your friends and family have their own as well. It's important to hold yourself accountable to achieve your goals and make yourself happy.

It's important to focus on your goal, but do not obsess over it. Keeping your journey productive but also fun will ensure you're motivated without overworking yourself. Sitting around and thinking about your goal all the time can cause you to burn out.

Your once-fun goal comes to feel more like a necessity than something you want to complete. Continue understanding how much you can do and improve upon to avoid burning out. Your mental approach is the key to success in any task you do.

Furthermore, success is still possible for everyone, no matter where they are in life. When you do, you can enable yourself to reset your life.

Whether you realize it or not, you have the capacity, ingredients and power to make a significant impact on the world over your lifetime.

Acknowledgments

I acknowledge my wife, Joanna Seymour, to whom I have been married for the past twenty-six years.

I also acknowledge our five children—Drexanna, Jowell, Drexwell, Josiah, and Jostin—with whom God has blessed me and put me in the position of father.

Let's Connect

Drexwell Seymour

Author & Speaker

Find out more about by clicking on the following links

Official Website

www.drexwellseymour.com

Instagram

www.Instagram.com/drexwellgseymour/

Linkedin

linkedin.com/in/drexwell-seymour-476b792a

Youtube

www.youtube.com/@drexwellseymour4634

Facebook

www.facebook.com/drexwellseymour

www.ingramcontent.com/pod-product-compliance
Lightning Source LLC
LaVergne TN
LVHW020648100826
845148LV00012B/2374
* 9 7 8 1 6 3 7 6 5 3 7 0 8 *